Shortly before her death C.D. Wright finished editing *ShallCross,* a collection that brings brief poems together with the longer forms for which she has become so recognized and beloved. Pushing the boundaries of genre, language, and poetic populism, *ShallCross* showcases a singular voice that navigates a rigorous space between journalistic activism, stunning narrative, sociopolitical outrage, and erotic lyricism. Comprising seven poetic sequences—including a collaborative suite written in response to photographic documentation of murder sites in New Orleans—*ShallCross* is further evidence that C.D. Wright is the most thrilling and innovative poet of the past four decades.

C.D. WRIGHT, SANTIAGO, CHILE, JANUARY 2016
PHOTOGRAPH BY FORREST GANDER

SHALLCROSS

C.D. WRIGHT
SHALLCROSS

COPPER CANYON PRESS

PORT TOWNSEND, WASHINGTON

Cover art: Denny Moers, *Farm Structures II*, 1997

Copper Canyon Press is in residence at Fort Worden State Park in Port
Townsend, Washington, under the auspices of Centrum. Centrum is a
gathering place for artists and creative thinkers from around the world,
students of all ages and backgrounds, and audiences seeking extraordinary
cultural enrichment.

LIBRARY OF CONGRESS CATALOGING-IN-PUBLICATION DATA
Names: Wright, C. D., 1949–2016.
Title: Shallcross / C.D. Wright.
Description: Port Townsend, Washington : Copper Canyon Press, [2016]
Identifiers: LCCN 2015043519 | ISBN 9781556594960 (hardback)
Subjects: | BISAC: POETRY / American / General.
Classification: LCC PS3573.R497 A6 2016 | DDC 811/.54—dc23
LC record available at http://lccn.loc.gov/2015043519

98765432 FIRST PRINTING

COPPER CANYON PRESS
Post Office Box 271
Port Townsend, Washington 98368
www.coppercanyonpress.org

GRATEFUL ACKNOWLEDGMENT TO:

"Some Old Words Were Spoken": *Conjunctions* #51, *The Death Issue.*

40 Watts: No, a journal of the arts #7, and Octopus Books.

Breathtaken (with linocuts by Walter Feldman): Brown Ziggurat Press.

Extract from *Breathtaken* (with photographs by Deborah Luster): *Conjunctions* #55, *Urban Arias.*

Extract from Breathtaken and "ShallCross": *Lana Turner: A Journal of Poetry and Opinion* #7.

The Other Hand: Horse Less Press.

"The Shearline of Obscurity" was composed for a collaboration titled *Spillforth* with Rick Hirsch, Michael Rogers, Gary Schnackenberg, and Forrest Gander.

"Obscurity and Providence" and "Obscurity and Lockdown": *PLUME* #3.

"Obscurity and the Amateur," "Tree of Obscurity," and "Obscurity and Operation Upshot-Knothole": *The American Poetry Review.* Bows, with respect to the third poem, to Rudolph Herzog's *A Short History of Nuclear Folly,* which along with Jonathan Schell's *The Fate of the Earth* has properly and indelibly given me the we-all-fall-down radioactive horrors.

"*from* The Obscure Lives of Poets": *Poetry.* Italicized lines are by William Wordsworth and Forrest Gander.

"Obscurity and Snow": *The New Republic,* April 24, 2015.

The form of "Obscurity and Legacy" was suggested by Pura Lopéz Colomé's "Fábula disuelta, ensimismada."

Poems from *The Other Hand* also appeared in: *American Poet; Lana Turner: A Journal of Poetry and Opinion; Lines in Long Array: A Civil War Commemoration, Poems and Photographs* (Smithsonian Books); and *The New Yorker*.

"Imaginary August" was published as a broadside at Baylor University (Beall Festival); "Imaginary August," "Imaginary Morning Glory," and "Imaginary June" were included in *Language Lessons* (Third Man Editions).

"Imaginary Hollywood," "Imaginary Suitcase," and "Imaginary México": *Volt* #20.

"Imaginary Waterfall": *Poetry London* #79.

"Closer": Gagosian Gallery and Aperture and *Harper's Magazine* for *Proud Flesh* by Sally Mann.

40 Watts is for Brecht. "Obscurity and Empathy" is for Toni. "Obscurity and Regret" and "Obscurity and Shelter" are for Brecht. "Obscurity and Elegance" is for Sharon. "Obscurity and Selfhood" and "Obscurity and the Amateur" are for Forrest. "Obscurity and Winter Sun" is for Michael. "Imaginary June" is for Susie.

for Forrest

line, lank and long,

be with

Be Still. The Hanging Gardens were a dream

TRUMBULL STICKNEY

CONTENTS

SHALLCROSS

SOME OLD WORDS WERE SPOKEN

Some Old Words Were Spoken

beside the hole, a photograph was

taken in which everyone is seen

touching everyone else. In the light

unmoving I lie, fixed on a stationary

sky of birds flying upside down

over a hill gone deep in its coloring.

Amid weird collisions of feeling

and gladioli, first and foremost, I want

to thank my dearest adversary for

putting a fire up under my words, for

releasing my husband when a stunned

fish emerged from an aqueous pit,

spit on his hands, and threw his old

house out the window. Thanks to those

who exposed the hairy, buff eggs

of my anxieties, their pupae of little

hypocrisies ¡Bravo! I say to the one

who pulled the shivering rug from

my bones, he who knelt over my face

drenched in self-inflicted tears, tendered

his pen and left me spinning the poetry

of white hair in advance of its years,

left me mouthing the sticky clusters

of regret, talking to a god in whom none

believe, then took me over the edge

of enchantment, my thanks. To the child

who refused to abdicate his ecstasy,

¡Encore! Between hammer and nail gun,

an ear is caressed by the sweet quibbling

Spanish of roofers through a scrim

of firs. Otherwise no one here but me

to break the frame, gnashing quietly.

For dying this way is a snap: no menus,

no wine lists, no taxis, no tickets,

no bulging duffel riding a conveyor belt

in the wrong capital; no one waiting

at the gate with a hand-lettered

sign. No, in fact, destination in mind.

Just an unseasonable chill. For dying

this way is nothing. Is like losing

a sock. A photograph is being set up

by my friend, the wedding photographer,

in which everyone is touching

everyone else and then everyone drifts off

into separate cars trailing swirls of dust.

(An unidentified observer reports that the caravan drove from
Ultima Thule to Paraclifta where they found nothing but a
string of catfish heads hung on a wire and some doves flying
around an abandoned gymnasium.)

40 WATTS

It is best
to take the uninformed
approach
look at the rock
how firm it stands
yet when the rain
touches its sides
how the hidden colors
show
it is best we tell our sons nothing

BESMILR BRIGHAM

Poem with Evening Coming On

a dog has appeared at the gate
for the second day in a row
against a dirty peach sky
a single car wobbles into the sun

Light Bulb Poem

at 4 o'clock I am at the door
with a bare hand of snow
laughing shamelessly
I undo my shirt
we'll pick up at the next chapter
my beloved are the words
of the rambler
if not the words the substance
the snow smeared across my front
warm to the touch
though we remain separated
as if by a chair
and I unwilling to read ahead

Café at the Junction Poem

the way he sees her
how the rain doesn't let up

forever blue and vigilant
an illuminated clock on the wall

peeling the label from her bottle
hungry but not touching her fish

curled over his wheel he turns
from the familiar route

where the trees hover over
the blacktop where the old orphanage

burned and she is trapping
a cross spider under a glass

Country Station Poem

it goes something like this: when the dog
lunged she froze he fired at the head

they drove around they came back he wore black
they line-danced they drank they fell down

they swore allegiance to the women who bore them
they cursed the women who bore them

the chambers of the heart opened and shut
they made plans they made plans

Poem with Undergrowth and Two Figures

If it rained today they would not go
to Wolf Spring. They would stay
inside the glass house on the lake.
Not see the black snake stretched
over the road. Not see the horse
and rider disappear into the drenched
tones of foliage. Not come upon
the clearing where the stench
of a dead animal quells the sound
or the smoke-streaked glimpse of her
boiling clothes in an iron pot.

Poem Taking Place before Lights Were Electrified

A man at a round table, his work boot
heeled on the rung of his chair,
his head in a black plate of blood.
I could see the bottle and the pan bread
through the blazing pine knots;
I watched the man who just shot him
walk the puncheon floor
bellowing *My brother, my blood...*
hoist the man onto his back
and stumble into a fine, filthy snow.

Amarillo Poem

A room across from a sporting house. With the dark,
I watched a woman washing the men off; then herself
she washed with a different cloth. It was fall. I was sitting
on my bed in my flame-proof gown. Every morning
I had to jump aboard my suitcase to get it to close.

Poem in Which Blood Flows

They are like brothers but
they know no filial feeling
and keep things in culverts.
As the tires on their trucks sink
into the heavy loam they spill
out of the pool hall's green light
into a plashing crescendo of blades.

Poem with a Cloudburst

the breath of the father
rises and falls

laundry blowing out of a basket
a gar is wrapped up

in some line the mind of the mother
snags on a compound word

such as *horsehair*
or *cottonwood*

on the meaning of the color yellow
it must be Sunday

Day-Old Widow Poem

he smiles as if but is not breathing
a moment ago he was in his chair
reading she was lighting the fire
she thought she heard a book
drop to the floor he didn't answer
in an instant she sensed it
a tangible space across an opening
she could neither enter nor fill
as if his eye hit upon a passage
elegant and cruel and true

Poem in Which the Lover

wakes in darkness of morning
and visits the water

lowering his glad body
onto a rock

the spiders rearrange
themselves underneath

Poem of a Houseboat Stranded in a Field

you have a beautiful white dresser
a quilt made by hand and a cat
who follows you inside and out
I've brought a liter of burgundy
and the sheet music you ordered
do you even know how fortunate
you are come on now girl give us
a little smile show us those teeth

Kind of Blue Poem

whatever she was overcoming
night issued out of night
until a cold wedge of light cut in

with both feet planted in mud

if she leaned over far enough
her hair hung over her knees
she hears shadflies hatching

This Much I Know Poem

I know I know this much
hair is hair a beer is a beer
is a beer and the next thing
crazy is as crazy does
furthermore tiger does not eat
tiger and bear will not bite bear
furthermore at present
the white elephant is extinct
nevertheless

Outlier's Poem

I have seen such things as they occur
in some remote and improbable time
with my eyes shut depending
on visibility depending on my receptivity
the raw fumes of some wildness
overtake a herd of cars all this
while the guests are in their bibs
polishing off the tails and green wine

Her Toes Poem

a ladder left out all winter
a wasp nest in a cornice
a rag mop and a girl they called Birdie
due to their dark hues
her clothes seem heavy and dense
her feet have not put on the shoes
huddled together by the bed
we are already in position
in the upper branches
for a backdrop her sheets
wrinkled stiff on the line

Poem Waiting for Sleep

on a night like this
craven, cavernous
all certainties desert her
the fire is dying
the fire is dead
deep down, deep inside
she sees nothing

Pure Sensation Poem

looking at the splintered floor
the square nailheads
the balls of dirt between the boards
one whorl in the wood
lets him feel invincible
as if on metal wings
sometime during the night
without noticing
he passes a sizable stone

Soldiers' Home Poem

she has been driving since
she woke up but she is lost now
in a tangle of trees
the overbearing smear of greens
then, an unmarked lane, poplars
on a bench a man
of indeterminate years
missing most of one side of him

Poem with Some Water Damage

She kept boarders kept hens
in the heart of town
heard birds whenever I phoned
now bullhorn now chopper
someone puts a plate in her hands
hours later someone takes the plate
from her hands *Damn* he says
if it isn't overcast again

Dog Put Down in Fall Poem

when they drive home in the evening
and the hound is not at the door
they head back to the car
and look for a café
with a lot of locals and noise
so they don't have to talk
or make eye contact and a table
near the window where
they can watch the scenery blur

Poem with a Dead Tree

it is late afternoon
she avoids looking
in its direction
she can feel
it moving toward her
in shaky black lines

Poem from Pearl's House

I can smell the lilacs
outside her window
I can smell the spring
where she kept things
cold I smell the shed
his worn-out leather
the snake that must've
been sleeping when
the rags hit the gasoline

Poem with a Dozen Cherries on a Ledge

a woman sweeping moths from a corner
straw coming out of the broom in handfuls
the violently blue sky

Water Baby Poem

frittering away the twilight
on the borrowed cycle, off the path,
she hears a small splashing, memory
of *when,* cherished sound of *him*
in an inflatable pool, naked, singing,
I'm naked, he sings, *Naked, I'm naked tonight*

Poem Missing Someone

shielding her eyes from the sun
with her free hand stabbed by
the sudden thought of him
standing on the rim of some pond
wind washing the beans out of his dish
teaching a dog to retrieve in water
living within himself one lost valley

Poem with No Up or Down

she is telling her husband that he is dead
and he is telling her he is no such thing
she tells him where he is buried and he
assures her that he is seated directly across
the table from her she tells him
she is going to call their son and settle this
then he'll need to cough up $$$ for rent

Poem with a Dart of Color

stopped getting the bottled
water then the paper cut off
the phone stopped buying
sunflower seeds essentially
went off grid yet the goldfinch
was back inspecting
her afflicted face
through the unwashed glass

Poem in Which Every Other Line Is a Falsehood

they walk around in the stubble
of the field sharing a winesap
after he cut his firewood he liked to sit
on a big log and listen to his blood rush
she turns her head in time to see
a flatiron float through an open window

Poem with a Girl Almost Fifteen

a name is scribbled over and over
in a notebook
a nest set fire to
larvae chew wool in a drawer
the hen rides her shoulder
to the mailbox

Poem from the End of Old Wire Road

hands as heavy as rocks
in the pockets of a Goodwill coat
kicking up leaves
she uncovers four trout lilies
Ah spring how it made her
want to walk backwards
or stick a fork in her side

Poem in a Trance

a boy is climbing stairs in his underwear
his flashlight shines in all directions
he stops in a doorway and turns it on his mother
a cloud of moths flutter over her shoulders
quiet and white as cells

Poem with a Missing Pilot

a piano is being moved
by someone not listening
to the rain from one end
of the room to another
a stale cigarette is filched
from a uniform before
the parakeets are let go

Poem in Which Her Mortgage Comes Due

the folds of a dark brown dress
the knuckles of a hand spent in dishwater
the jars of rhubarb
the folios of poetry
the suitcase filled with worthless notes
the fiery fields
the fields on fire

Back Forty Poem

a barn held up by a pitchfork
surrounded by field on field
of wildflowers, butterflies,
cow pies, beyond which
the snake-infested woods
the high-voltage fence
the big-stripe inmates

Rooming House Poem

from the dusk's long windows
the boy follows the man
in the felt hat walking briskly toward
Daddy Joe's bond and car lot

Downtown in January Poem

the cold is in our shoes
the first trillion pins of snow
strike the statue's field glasses
a branching line forms
in sycamore light
blare of sudden color among the coats
moving at odd angles in the plaza
where a glove was dropped
over a year ago

Poem Starved for Music

the room itself anonymous
no object is mundane
a hairy rope in a box
a pair of bifocals
on a chenille bed the cat
watches me smoke
waiting for it to cool off
a pair of skinny ghosts
we go rambling

Poem without Angel Food

Well, a great many things have been said
in the oven of hours. We have not been
shaken out of the magnolias. Today was another
hard day. And tomorrow will be harder. Well,
that sounds like our gong. But we'll have
the boy's birthday and we will have
music and cake. Well, I will think only
good thoughts and go up and talk to the rock.

Poem of a Forest of Clouds Sweeping By

your life blew past as a shirt off a line
but then turned and turned again
O Archangel of the Mirror
what would you have done
it's been said that over the years
the house sustained the smell
of fresh-cooked trout and the rest
as we well know is still journeying

BREATHTAKEN

For the purposes of this writing, I was a self-appointed gleaner from the NOLA.com Crime Blog, under the lead of Brendan McCarthy with contributions from an extended cast of reporters for the *Times-Picayune*. The crime section of the site also maintains a day-to-day murder map. And St. Anna's Episcopal Church on Esplanade posts on its front lawn a murder board it endeavors to keep up. The homicides referred to were not exclusive to but were concentrated in a period of two years. A few individuals who lost loved ones to violence were very informally interviewed by this writer: Nakita and Yolande Shavers, sister and mother of Dinerral Shavers whose accused 17-year-old murderer three weeks after his acquittal was rearrested on a new attempted murder charge; the mother and aunt of Paul Ellis, 16, shot 29 times by four shooters with no arrests made; and Rose Preston, author of the *Crime Victims Guidebook,* whose husband and mother-in-law were brutally murdered by her mother-in-law's tenants. One of their killers died in the Parish jail of a ruptured ulcer. Charges were dropped against the other perpetrator after she participated in a restorative justice process.

Many individuals and civic, city, and faith organizations stand against the ruthless ravaging of the City That Care Forgot. I would single out Silence Is Violence at the Sound Café for being such an effective, dedicated center and umbrella for Orleanians trying to repair and reclaim their distinctive, beautiful lives. Thanks also for the edifying and soul-nourishing lunches occasionally nabbed with Mary Howell at Luizza's by the Track.

This project was conceived as a corollary to photographer Deborah Luster's *Tooth for an Eye: A Chorography of Violence in Orleans Parish.*

I fear…
And so…
It's terrible…
Bear with…

Breathtaken

i.

napping   in her car with her 19-week fetus

at the tattoo parlor   behind the barbershop

in a coffee-colored shotgun, Seventh Ward   a triple

                              one of the men wore women's clothes

in the chest by a neighbor

under a cell tower

during a concert at Hush

next to a snowball stand

in a trash bin   facedown

in the shadow of the Superdome

facedown   she brought a flower to the spot

in the driver's seat

fleeing   into Sleepy's Lounge

while walking down Chippewa, 8:20 p.m.

                              she had on the dress he bought her

facedown

bringing back stuff to make gumbo

lying on his back on Willow   watching the dark torsos of clouds

shots sprayed from a green van

working on a house   he loved his mother's pies

by his idling car

faceup   watching the clouds bulk up and blow over

in the passenger seat on Sister Street

walking home, 5:25 p.m.   carrying a bottle of whole milk

in a room at the Travelodge   pending identification

in the family living room   watching his program

parked in his pickup   half a muffuletta in his lap

beneath a tree   looking up through a canopy of speckled light

in a pile of debris   outside a blighted house

faceup   the sun severed by rebar

after being carjacked the night before   his girlfriend

after they raped her they shot her   Hush

one spoke   through a slot in his stockinet

inside his apartment   in his favorite shirt

from a black Acura

felled on Constance

while changing a flat on I-10 eastbound

in the stairwell   of an Algiers complex

on Josephine on Christmas night   a double

on the sidewalk on St. Ann   wearing counterfeit Nikes

facedown   he tried to avoid the cracks in the walk

beside a bicycle   a thin chevron of hair above the lip

side entrance of St. Luke's

last seen leaving a club   in the Sugar District

inside his water-damaged apartment   a witness

to a murder trial postponed

                    [first the killer had to drop off his kids]

ii

corner of Hollygrove and Palm

over the Industrial Canal on Chef Menteur

lying on Olive Street   looking at the moon

swollen, urinous

inside a silver Isuzu

corner of Touro and N. Roman

at the former Sugar Bowl Lanes   decomposed

near Elysian Fields overpass

in the backyard   watching the rags of cloud float over

driving north

driving a black Buick Regal

driving on Felicity

on the sidewalk about noon

                                                        clouds

pushing past   the lenses of his Ray-Bans

in the courtyard of a housing complex   near the struggling live oak

N. Roman again   hushed

inside a red Chevy Lumina

in the Community Care   Psychiatric Hospital

after being stomped and beaten   and forsaken

facing   a mud nest under a gallery

on Dauphine

in the backyard   wearing counterfeit True Religion jeans

in the front yard

Calyisse, 19, and Fitzgerald, 19

                        in an abandoned house near Fig Street

in Gert Town   home of Blue Plate Mayonnaise Factory

                                                elevation 0

iii

[*Fabulous*, that was her byword]

inside a black Toyota Scion

inside her ransacked house

inside Happy Jack Social and Pleasure Club

lying in the street   facing

                        a deflated basketball under a parked car

iv

N. Prieur again

in his FEMA trailer   asleep with the TV on

in the Tallowtree neighborhood

inside his home with his throat slit

                              [by gunshot unless otherwise noted]

in his house on Terpsichore

on Claiborne at the line   between Pigeon Town and Hollygrove

New Year's Day

                        in front of his grandmother's house, Sixth Ward

shot 14 times   [courtesy of NOPD]

at a graduation party in the backyard

                                    a girl totally in love with poetry

mother of a 30-month-old   the father ambushed in his car

a few days after she learned she was pregnant

he never even knew   [her cycle was off]

by men in black   coming out from the trees shooting

in a car chase

sprawled   out of a black Chevrolet Monte Carlo

twins   on Telemachus and Baudin

under a vehicle   from a beating

intersection of Conti and Treme

in the Holy Cross neighborhood

in Le Petit Motel   an unidentified woman

in the 8200 block of Chef Menteur

at Cooper public housing

next to an abandoned complex in St. Roch   [found by a dog]

at Cooper public housing again   his mama is going to miss him

something awful

on Elysian Fields

on Touro again

found in her pickup

former NOPD   near Downman Rd. ramp

in a baby blue Volkswagen   talking

through the car window   smoke gushing out of her nostrils

at Iberville again

in the back of the head   near The Commons Bar in a Cardinals cap

homeless, stabbed in torso

homeless, stabbed in back

on Loyola

on Danzinger Bridge, a boy, 17   in the back [NOPD]

on Danzinger Bridge, a man, mentally challenged

                                        in the back [NOPD again]

behind the wheel of his new car

by a peer, 14

on Babylon Street, 17, by peers

in Gert Town   elevation 0

home to Blue Plate Mayonnaise Factory

playing dice on the porch   a triple

three more still breathing   Lower Ninth

Jack's Bus Stop

near the Super Sunday parades

in town to visit relatives for Memorial Day

                                        when he stayed in Houston

he was out of the woods   so his mama thought

in Terrytown   named for the developer's first girlchild, a triple

near intersection of Old Gentilly Rd.

                                        and Michoud, found beside the road

Brittany, 17   [who never met a stranger]

the baby would not stop crying

                              multiple fractures and rends in the anus

in the Ninth Ward, a double

in St. Roch near intersection of Johnson   and Music

N. Claiborne and Frenchmen

Wendy a bartender at Aunt Tiki's and   Starlight by the Park

corner of Governor Nicholls and Dauphine   by three teens

[turned in by the parents]

his shredded heart   feeling death upon him

the evidence voluminous

I put her body in water I'm willing to give

                              you that the prisoner replied

That other, that's a grey area

[he was said to get off watching

                    their eyes roll to the back of their head]

a preponderance of evidence requires   a lower standard than proof

beyond a reasonable doubt

once you start talking about   more than one murder

and the defendant is ugly to look at

                              ugly acting or has an ugly history

in water   evidence such as semen

can be ruined by marine life

the Handcuff Muzzle™ is an effective

                              and versatile restraint device

the Handcuff Muzzle™ is made of   vented mesh nylon

                    [this material has a long life expectancy]

this material is washable and comes   in a variety of colors

the Grommet guarantees a snug fit

in two main sizes   one is for securing females or males

with smaller hands

the other size   your general population

an X-large bag   by special order

the Wrap is the ultimate immobilization system

[never think upwards   unless downwards first]

it's police blotter time   Did you lock the side door

                                                Well, I said, Hell to yes

v

inside a white Chevy Impala

in the rear of Fischer public housing complex

on the side of abandoned Kennedy High

lying in an alley next to an abandoned house   faceup

                                                dreaming of electric sheep

vi

hushed   in a robbery

in a struggle   with a man

being questioned   [that was Cotton]

inside Exclusive Cuts   [Consuelo]

run down by a car driven   by his daughter's boyfriend

in a rented Pontiac

in New Edition Bar

in Friar Tuck's Bar

at Club Fabulous

at Club Desire   on Law and Desire

in Pal's Bar, Bayou St. John   her 28-year-old throat slashed

by a man on his way out the door   [that was Nia]

at the Crescent City Connection

at Show Stopper Tattoos   in back of Spice One

outside the Chat Room

in an overgrown lot   in the neighborhood of Desire

partially charred   [that was Jody]

on Piety

between two vacant houses   the light there has an aura

the smell of sweet olive   so strong

near the corner of Amelia

St. Roch again, a double   before lunchtime

on the sidewalk, faceup   he beheld

a confusion of color

in front of a gutted house   Lower Ninth

Porche was her name

near the tracks

in a FEMA trailer   the9thwardwordman

thence   his mama entered a conglomerate of hurt

vii

while walking   down Frenchmen about 9:15

on the sidewalk on Lotus near Myrtle

in a grassy area in the Iberville complex

on Frenchmen, again   Dominique, 16

in the middle of the street   near the Black Pearl

Treme   Marquise, 20, Sylvester, 17

on Laharpe   a triple

lying on the street staring at the asphalt moon

under an abandoned house, a French citizen

in Lake Pontchartrain   newlyweds

another on Pleasure Street   in a burning car

on Sunday on Cadillac

on the steps of her Irish Channel home

in a blue Olds on S. Roman, on a porch, N. Roman

eating a raw potato

faceup   looking at the marbled clouds

the 16th this year, on St. Claude   [we're hardly done with June]

when he fell, when she saw him fall   his mama vomited

viii

in March   two families

on Clouet [Angel; her children, Jamaria, 7

                                        Joseph, 4; her sister Malekia, 17]

in Treme   two Muses:

Jennifer, her sister Monica;   her mother Wanda

under the steps of the porch   of a lime-colored shotgun

ix

a triple   on Laharpe

three men dressed in black

on the sidewalk, 2500 block of Upperline

among a cluster of trailers

on the sidewalk in the Seventh Ward   from that angle of repose

he could make out the cages

of his mother's Creole tomatoes

crashed   into a handicapped-access ramp

a witness who testified against Bonds

stuffed inside a Metro can   in the Bywater

the Wild Man of the FiYiYi Mardi Gras Indians   his girlfriend

a short-order cook   in a parked car

near the Crescent City Connection

rammed and shot on S. Claiborne   a suspect in another shooting

on N. Tonti   a double

one down on Pleasure St., again

two in one day   on Lizardi

three on Josephine

in Hollygrove, again   a drum major

his countenance drained of dread   and his characteristic optimism

gone flat   [no one dying to live on Josephine]

x

breathtaken

in the Faubourg Marigny   beaten, burned

dumped in the woods on Dwyer Rd.   he was going into the city

to take care of some business   he told his mama

he would be back   later

yesterday a boy, 17   in the Fair Grounds

this morning, faceup   bleeding out by a light pole

at Terpsichore   [in view of customers

from a convenience store   a clump of uniformed students

a man sitting on his stoop tells   the cub reporter

There's just too much going on around here.]

                    You are listening to The Problem Child.

                    It's hot and humid. Overcast again.

Petition to the Bearers of Precious Images
to recollect a few things about him/her

How long ago did you lose your loved one   to this violence
Where was your loved one taken
What time of year, what hour
What was your loved one's relation to you

What was your loved one's given name
Did you have a pet name for your loved one
If you knew your loved one as a child   could you
Pass on a precious image   to a mere bystander to bear
What was your loved one's best physical feature
Could you draw that feature blind
Did your loved one have a sweet tooth
What was your loved one's prized possession
Did you keep a piece of your loved one's clothing
Was your loved one a day person or a night person
Was your loved one a good mimic
Was your loved one a good loser
Did your loved one like beets or rhubarb   or okra or gizzards
Hog jowls [with or without greens]
Did your loved one have a name for you other than your given
Did your loved one ever catch an eel   barehanded
Could your loved one stand on her head
Do you have any pictures made by him
Did your loved one like to read
Could your loved one tell a story
Was that your loved one's burgundy bike
Did your loved one like the movies
Was there something in school that for
Your loved one was extra
Did your loved one know any lyrics
Did your loved one play a mouth harp
Did your loved one own a gun
Was there anything your loved one liked   to collect
After your loved one was taken   is there anything
Anyone told you about them   [that took you by surprise]
Did your loved one have long feet

Did your loved one have pretty ears
Did your loved one like pockets
Did your loved one wear his hair   in a special way
Did your loved one ever do something   just for you
That made you feel extra
Could your loved one swim on his back   dance, drive
A big piece of machinery
Was your loved one a fast runner   a fast talker
Did your loved one like snowballs   tabasco, poboys
Did you say your loved one lies   in the Garden of Memories
Or is she with Our Lady Queen of Peace
Could your loved one tell a joke
What was your loved one's best color
If your loved one was a hurter   can you
Pass a night with feelings   other than regret
Can you lift yourself up
If your loved one never hurt a bug
Can you pass a day without rancor   can you
Lift yourself up   again

THE OTHER HAND

I have in some subtle sense to fight my hand if
I am to grow along the reaches of my nerve.

ANNE TRUITT

Obscurity and Empathy

The left hand rests on the paper.

The hand has entered the frame just below the elbow.

The other hand is in its service.

The left moves along a current that is not visible
and on a signal likewise inaudible, goes still.

For the hand to respond the ink must be black.

There is no watermark.

One nail is broken well below the quick.

The others filed short.
Or chewed.

The hand is drawn to objects.

In another's it becomes pliant
and readily absorbs the moisture of the other's.

It retains the memory of the smell of her infant son's hair.

Everything having been written, the hand has to work hard
to get up in the spaces.

There is no tremor, but the skin is thin and somewhat
crepey.

The veins stand out.

The hand has begun to gesture toward its ghosthood.
Though at times it becomes almost frisky.

The desk is side-lit.

The hand has options, but has chosen to stay
inside its own pale, thin walls.

It has begun to show signs of its own shoddy construction.

The hand is there to express shouts and whispers,
ordinary love,

the afterimage of everything.

From the outside what light leaks through the blind
is blue, blue-grey.

There is a dog.

There is a fan.

The fan is on the dog.

Obscurity and Regret

The hand without the glove screws down the lid

on the jar of caterpillars, but the apple trees

are already infested. The sun mottles

the ground. The leaves are half-dead.

A shoe stomps the larvae streaming

onto the lawn as if putting out a cigarette on a rug.

It was a stupid idea. It was a stupid thing to say,

the thought belonging to the body says to its source,

stomping on the bright green grass as it spills its sweet guts.

Obscurity and Elegance

Whether or not the park was safe

she was going in. A study concluded, for a park

to be successful there had to be women.

The man next to the monument must have broken

away from her. Perhaps years

before. That the bond had been carnal is obvious.

He said he was just out clearing his head.

They followed the walk of pollarded pears. His tone

distant but not disinterested. It was

an expensive suit, she could tell by the cut.

His face blocked by the felted hat. The cocked night

studded with satellites. Women

were known not to enter a park

if they smelled urine. They passed under the arch

together. At this point, he allowed, it

would be fine by him if he could sit at his desk

and watch his writing happen.

The Shearline of Obscurity

Water

Cold as it sounds

The storm glass

Refilled and sealed

With a wine cork

The spout spilling over

Ultramarine

Mixed with red

Producing

Black on black

The ravens absorb

During those evocations, those divinations of the observer

Of the interplay between shades

Breathe, rest, wait, keep silent

Walk toward the bay swinging the arms

Abandon sandals at the end of the blacktop

To cross the dredged up stratum of sand

To stand at the edge expecting

To go totally blind

Upon seeing a four-armed sea star regenerating

Obscurity and Shelter

it's the moon
it looks so natural
it's early yet
it's at the brink
it's still light
it's not too late
it's growing more insistent
it's the same house

that is incommunicado
I see a woman reading a book
they could walk to the water
of a memory she doesn't want to call up
trailing scarves of fog
blow between her eyes
the face is always there
skeletal but secure
where he grew up
a one-story clapboard with stuff
crammed into drawers
waiting for the adults to go out
never enough closets
so he could roll a smoke or call her
pull the door to
and start sprouting a mustache
who ate to the tail
straight from the fridge
trout skin flesh cartilage
always against everything
on multiple channels
as one's intentions are so often
obscured to oneself
wanting what one wants
the closeness, the warmth
that takes place before fire
a world before his candle
it's the ria that's heard
beyond the treeline

the water folding back
a blanket that waits
for the body
halflistening
overflowing
its archipelagoes
ria in Galician
drowned valley

Obscurity and Isolation

The left hand rests on the paper.

The hand has entered the frame just above the elbow
to reveal a half-rolled sleeve.

The other hand is in its service.

It holds a foggy glass up to a standing lamp.

Motel furniture. Motel paneling.

From the outside, what light slips through the blind
is grey, blue-grey.

The phone rings. The hand, conditioned to pick up,
hesitates, withdraws

before the ringing finally breaks off;

Obscurity and Providence

The hand is immobilized

so the hand not usually in use

has to do all the work, has learned

to wait, to be quiet, to be still,

to receive memories; to tend

the fire; sometimes perceiving

a vague presence, the hand extends

in the perceived direction, retreats,

pulls a sheet of paper from the drawer

that sticks, wet or dry;

scribbling fast at last, *What*

is he doing now, now that it is cold

where does he sleep.

When the dressing comes off

the smell is really pug.

Obscurity and Selfhood

Not far
from a college.
Nevertheless.
A man
living by himself

kept his fighting cocks in plain sight. Each had its own tether and
miniature shed and dish with embossed sobriquet. Their domestication
reserved for battle before the table. *Gallus gallus domesticus.* A young
male, a cockerel, my husband's patronymic before the adoption. Some
hens
are disposed to poach another's egg. Once there were teeth. Given
certain
conditions they could come back. If not a full set. Even now a breathing
hole
has to be pipped for the offspring to break out. This is done with an egg
tooth.
Not a true tooth. Love among the chickens involves a circle dance. He is
a wonderful dancer. It goes straight to her brain. Before and after they
prefer
to wash off in dust. Ashes will work if no dust. If they aren't forced into
shedding
one another's blood, they can live until their heart gives out.
The cock
the man
could not
resist
loving.
He withdrew
from

the ring.
Yet
relinquished.
To settle
an unforgiven
debt.

My question is this:
Would you describe yourself
as a wanderer, a friend of the court, amicus curiae, falsely construed
as a snitch, a blue yodeler, an apostate, a lost cause, a bird in the
house, a biter, a common blogger, a contender, a purse snatcher,
a false witness, a palterer, a silkie, a backyarder, channeler for
malevolent spirits, girt in the loins, figure on a shard of black
pottery, moderately active, a fog machine, a visionary miserabilist,
a chook or a cuckold, a roundhead, a little seditious,

a slow-wave sleeper, a dead mule, a gongorist, honey on the comb,
half goat half god, a white throwback, crossed with a mongrel, a
genesis, a retired fighting
cock,
a doll
named
Memphis.

Obscurity and the Amateur

A glass is filled with white water from

the tap and carried to a shaky table under the pencil

tree where the glass gradually clears.

The rhododendron shouldn't have been planted under

the canopy but showed blooms this year.

A few throwaway lines are put down and rubbed out.

The arborist doesn't show up or call

to cancel. The chair sits low but the scrawl is adjusted

at the wrist. A book is being written

by an amateur for the lay. A legal pad held down

with a rock in the unlikely event

of a puff of air. Before long the mind sees a couple

making out against a stone wall;

the mind warns itself that love is not inborn so bends

toward the breaking point but love also

abhors a vacuum so gloms on to glimmers of not being

wholeheartedly blue. While maintaining

the profile of a raptor. It is a borderline experience.

Currents of doubt move around and

through. Behind the flawless motion of staggering

clouds, the sky. With great effort, an insect trails a leg

down the length of the table.

Obscurity and Velocity

Asleep in her chair, but
dreaming, heedless that she was
driving past the unfenced fields
in which constantly shifting greens
flowed in one direction; she was picking
up speed, leaning forward when something
in the background, something in partial shadow
snagged a tine of her attention, scanning stations; her foot
kept accelerating toward that gouged out mountain, or else

from **The Obscure Lives of Poets**

How is it that you live, and what is it you do?

WORDSWORTH, to the leech-gatherer

Three, no, four, that I know, married women
of means and brains. One grew moss on her tongue, waking from dreams that smelled
of mildew or hoary socks on a smothering train.
One turned to falconry and the construction of seed bombs to be dropped from three-
story houses. One burned her burka upon being released
from prison for the fourth time shamed so down deep in her molested self, washed
henceforth in formal darkness, another burned
her wedding dress in a fire pot while house finches splashed in the birdbath. [*how one
moment touches on another moment and a thought flickers on and off*]
One poet, obsessed with vulvae, son of a butcher,
displayed a large bezoar on his coffee table, and slept in the bear nests in the Ardèche,
obsessed. One poet, adopted shortly after birth
by a levee builder on the St. Francis, shot himself with a target pistol on a beautiful
afternoon in early June. One lay across the tracks
on the brink of the Tiananmen uprising. One picked up her manuscript, a block of ash,
from the embers of her Oakland home. Bakhtin, as we know,
smoked his very best pages in prison. The poems of Radnóti were found by his widow in
his overcoat, in a mass grave. One scribbled until his last
conscious breath in an apartment in Waltham, brimmed over with hellish fury and
dysfunctional passion. One was imprisoned on a ship
in Valparaiso during the military coup, but lived with his "iron bad health" to carve a poem
3.5 kilometers long in the Atacama desert,
and another in the skies over Brooklyn; to cover thousands of pages with anguish and
light. One is fascinated with lichens and other symbionts.
One with fungi and other entheogens. [*how the divine is elusive and pelf is conspicuous*]
One spent the better part of this life
writing in the dirt with a stick, crossing out with his foot, that his entire tribe could
decipher the mystery inscribed. [Another *surrendered
his youth and gladness with lines of despondency and madness.*] One broke faith with the word
before the word could break faith with her, and built
a mountain of detergent in her garage. One made a record of night-flying birds on a scroll
longer than the roll of post-Katrina homicides
in Orleans Parish. One does not like white flowers and has never
shown her poems to a single solitary living soul. Another built a pair of metal wings to be
worn once and then pressed between the covers
of a golden book. One joined the Int'l Concatenated Order of the Hoo Hoo but
absconded for Europe where he lives large
as an unaffiliated psychedelic narcissist. Some just want the big life. Others suffer
into the night at the thought of what
they should have said, *un autre esprit d'escalier.* One was able to buy his first car
after a settlement from being bit by a pit bull.
One resolved to trim her hair once she began to sit upon it. One walked alone from
Savannah to Santa Monica. The perfect time to read
the Bible and *Gravity's Rainbow.* One posed under a tortuosa beech at Arnold
Arboretum when her picture was taken; wrote
longhand crossing the Gulf, got a job statuing in New Orleans. One of the venerated
continues to write though his sight has abandoned
him and his garden is returning to wilderness. One snores and never locks her doors.
One has lamellar ichthyosis and did not shed her collodion
membrane. Rare relief springs from poetry and lying flat, cloud-searching on the grass.
[*how a glass ear is fashioned from words*]
One poet goes silent as fishes; one stands in a lightning field and slowly begins to move.
[*As a fugue composed in an open boat*]
One writes again every thousand+ days and plants all things magenta, so named
for the Italian town of that name.
One, as a lock against beggary and death, writes only elegies; was advised by a mild elder:
It is all right to be depressed just as long
as you don't let it get you down. [how *wisteria can bring down a house / likewise cat's claw*]
One dreamed of leaving her colicky son
under the bleachers. One survived multiple tumors in his brain decades after a year-long
tour in Vietnam. Another walked off
the uranium fields, survived melanoma and many more unkind cuts, *torn awake.*
How here: [*The story has a skip in it. Listen, Señor, I have been used
by my own ignorance, self-disgust, my instinct for failure. Pray for me.*]
Seen in this light (this damnable dingy light),
Brothers and Sisters, Señors y Señoras, I tell you how it is that we live, and what it is that
we do, we get ourselves up, off our much abused sofas,
Hermanos, Hermanas, to the old intolerable sound of hollow spoons in hollow bowls,
to insure that our love has not left the world or else

Obscurity and Voyaging

The hand was having a hard time holding the pen.

A superficial cut.

A long clear silent night.

A book held open by a dolostone.

The occupant selects a sentence, *No one knows*
how small the smallest life is.

If there's a call, it will not be answered.

A bath, the burning of sweetgrass soothe the limbs.

As a memory stings the brain.

The furniture serviceable but weird, on the verge
of grotesque.

The vein of light under the door is a comfort
to the occupant.

The air inhales the passerine lines of a single singer.

A motorcycle saws through the song and goes.

An appliance purrs at intervals.

The pen was bought in Gubbio near
the thin band marking the great dying of dinosaurs.

The pen, a gift.

There
The tree just
Standing
There
The chestnut from which she descended
Leaf on leaf
Worm by worm
Snow on snow
Born for what resplendent reason
To irrigate this dumb mud
With his oblivious blood
Who always thought he would
Once
Again
Get up
After sucking her breast
After
Putting away his nibs
After
An unexceptional dinner with friends
Die in the snow

FROM THE BELLY OF A LAMB

Imaginary August

If one stood perfectly still. Even in the withering hours

of then. Hair down to here. Being alive and quiet.

One could forget oneself. Forget what one didn't even recognize.

How mad it felt. Subliminally. One could pick out goldfinches

and mourning cloaks among the dying stalks of cosmos,

and across the ditch of grey wastewater they use to irrigate

the burial ground, a young man in a late-flowering tree

taking our photograph.

Imaginary Hollywood

The set was on when she fell asleep

In black and white

a woman was gliding through a garden in period clothes

and a child was touching

a pane of wavy glass with the flat of her hand

Another woman

was all but flying down spiral stairs in a flouncy gown

that showed off

the cut of her breasts and a lone golden strand

of hair playing at her ear

It was because of… she didn't want to grow any older

her resistance

was strong the dream's spores hung in the air

in another room

a parent was dying in short shallowing breaths

she needed

somewhere to put all that emotional excess

that's the way

it was when she began talking in fake accents

sleeping late

as a lake to avoid as many hours of living

dread as if dread

could be outslept; the stretch limo

in her eleven-year-old

head wrapped itself around the corner

That's the way

it would be, everyone slender as drinking straws

nobody leaky

or hurting or abjectly religious, everything

allbillowyyellowyorangeyflowywonderfulness

Imaginary Morning Glory

Whether or not the water was freezing. The body
would break its sheath. Without layer on layer
of feather and air to insulate the loving belly.
A cloudy film surrounding the point of entry. If blue
were not blue how could love be love. But if the body
were made of rings. A loose halo would emerge
in the telluric light. If anyone were entrusted to verify
this rare occurrence. As the petal starts to
dwindle and curl unto itself. And only then. Love,
blue. Hallucinogenic blue, love.

Imaginary Waterfall

You could ask any one of them up by the lake
                                        It had presence

Fold of coldness folded over cold

The rumors of what was beyond
                                        mostly worthless

You had to take into account who was telling
                                        the story and

for whose ends

Against the dark of her intuition
                                        an unrelenting stream

of light starting to set like cement

some mildew tingeing the dream since

its uniform had not been
                                        properly kept

Where her love stood

until he stepped behind the overhang
                                        the synesthesia of his name

a silver helmet ringing
                                        when struck

Imaginary Suitcase

This belonged to your mother. Now

it is yours though you have no memory

of her and we'll never know if she wrote it

by herself or copied it down from a book.

In this pouch is a lock of her velvet hair.

Anyone on the square would tell you,

she was a beautiful girl. I know this won't

get you far but when you get to where

you're going, Youngblood, that your days

be long, and your nights release a fleet

of dreams, your love be a trumpet vine.

Pocket every penny that drops and swear off

the sauce that ate the head of your father.

Imaginary Rope

The visitor woke early as visitors are often
curious as to what will happen next
in the house of the host a white cat stalks
the low rock wall the room is just so
the visitor has slept as if inside a flower
there is a sense of having crossed
over an unhurried river where there was
a drawbridge but no operator and the undulant
grasses on the opposite bank emulate
the whish of a sleep application that could be
the rhythmic wash of rain or of some sinister
approach or the strain of an unutterable
weight from a swinging line of hemp

Imaginary June

Night: wears itself away   clouds too dense to skim
over the sheer granite rim   only a moment before
someone sitting in a mission chair   convinced   101%
convinced   she could see into her very cells
with her unassisted eyes   even into extremophiles
even with the light dispelled   until the mind sets sail
into its private interval of oblivion   a hand falls from its lap
a pen drops to a carpet   a stand of leaves whispers as if
to suggest something tender   yet a potentially heart-robbing
sequel: to a dream in which faces flare up   fuse   dissolve
but there is a lot of color before their vanishing   and a name
for such phenomena   that comes from the belly of a lamb
rather   not a lamb anymore   from the stomach
of a particular canny but kind: blind-from-birth ewe

Imaginary México

Naturally there would be frijoles tortillas habaneros and queso
there would be a man sharpening knives on a stationary bike
brass instruments and just this one time the absence of mariachis
narcos would be queued up in shackles hair swirling around
their navels generating a vortex straight to damnation no young
brutalized women no young dispossessed boys going through
the basura at the rusty trombone we would be moving supple
as a moray eel and secretive until borracho and burned
by a careless cigarette then only would our terrifying teeth
be exposed and a yellow taxi pull up to transport us back
to a hotel equipped with showers a thousand and one
times better than the one back home the water no more or less
potable the sins of our forebears transferable into perpetuity

CLOSER

Closer

Behold a man, the most familiar body outside one's own
(to which one pays less and less attention) as perfect in its
imperfections as in its perfections. Immobile at eye-level, faceless,
speechless, the body of the husband, the momentous nearness
of the body like something grafted to something not kin to
itself, and yet the graft has taken, the invisible areas seen into,
the visible obscured. What is he thinking? With his back half in
shadow. Or the dark being drawn off just below the navel. How
does it feel to go limp over the edge. The torso turning into a
crucible of light. To lie as a nautilus on an old duvet. Do they talk
during this *procedure*. What time is it? Does it matter? In this
night for day. Studio light. By day a flashing of wings past the
windows. There is a lot of glass. Some hit and drop with a barely
audible thud. The barrier of the medium conspicuous and at last
insignificant. So used are they to one another. The mechanical
activity scarcely noted. Like something grafted... This time spent
together doing this, photographing, being photographed. They
postpone the ending. No other body will do—he is not a figure.
This is not a life study, but a chronicle of *them*. They are in this
together. They are in this for the long haul. They haul. Food is
brought in. Firewood. Bills paid. The horses need them. The dogs
give more than they are given. Dogs being lavish in the ways
of love. The instrument is cold. Harsh even. But the care with
which it is leveled on this foot, the toes hammering, those weird
twin ovals in the background, handles to a cabinet. This flank,
where the wasting has scoured the thigh, buttock. The penis so
docile. It becomes the receptive organ. Because he does not need
to withhold. What time is it? What difference? Mayflies have
mere hours to get themselves out of the mud, mate, and die.

These two have until the end of hours. If he were to tell her he
was beginning to feel a draft, would she cover him or say, Wait,
I'm almost done. Don't move. Equally virile and vulnerable.
Would he ever complain. Does he ever drift off. Float above
himself. During this *procedure*. When one is no longer emerging
one is vanishing. Whether or not we loathe this paradox, we
carry it out. The aphrodisiac of silence. Then there is some talk,
not a lot. This has been going on a long time, these sessions, the
radio tuned to NPR. Since the last election. The fields green and
flowing, then brown and stubbled. Dusted white once or twice.
Less every year. The house lulled under an afternoon moon.
Sound of a hose being dragged, a barrow with a heavy load.
Smell of tack. They become reclusive. Her especially. He does the
shopping. He goes to an office. It is just the two of them now.
Certain sensations have to be attended, an itch that intensifies, an
ache that gets louder. The body assumes an impromptu position.
Some see-through material is hung up. Unbleached muslin or
an old tablecloth. Now stand behind that. Within hearing of a
branch cracking. Crows cawing. Always crows. Distant drone of
machinery. The light stretched, curved, squared off. The contrasts
strictly regulated. Stippling of the backs of the legs. Torn strips.
Craquelure. Shredding. Blackened slurry in the corner of the
frame. She did that. He is worn smooth, marmoreal. Tomorrow
he goes into town, to lawyer. If the room were amplified it would
tick and respirate as walls and windows disappeared. Tallowy
rags from the duvet. A bowl made by a friend, a Russian tea
glass, an aerial of a television disguised as blackdrop, and them.
A man beheld. It goeth to the quick. Has your arm gone to
sleep? The way they knew it would be. How is it their privacy is
not penetrated by the audacity of our stare? How is it that these
frames add up to an enactment, not a series of stills of him? Let's

all sit down in our broken chairs with our broken hearts in our lap and clap. Anticipation of movement, of a sudden shift. The body's betrayal, dignified by its bearing. Just some light, some cloth, a worktable, a man lying or standing with his foot on a stool. *The mystery,* wrote the woman, *in how little we know of other people, is no greater than the mystery of how much.* The converse is also true. Do you need to stretch now? Can you open your legs more? Were you dreaming? If she knew what he was thinking, would she turn away. Every frame, evidence of deep true

Control. Clear, beautiful, frozen. Would she turn away. Never.

SHALLCROSS

ShallCross

We are walking along a curve

Observed by the hawk

Completing the arc

For us but not by us

Responding to the gravity

Of the bend as we climb

Toward a jagged ridge

Pages fluttered by the softest

Wind as wind slips through

The folding door

Of a listing phone booth

Across the drawbridge

A store called Her Hands

A club called His Room

An out-of-date flier for

A free seminar for the heart

Angelica is rampant

Egrets flock the treetops

The day wears itself away

Against the barbed fencing

A barge goes quietly off course

Cars are sparser now

Crows are everywhere

Getting bigger louder closer

In a well-kept farmhouse

A lid slams down

On a pounded piano

As the words sink into me

You are still young enough

To adopt a xolo

Write an opera on glass

Bed a chimera

Bedazzle and be devoured

The moonroof in your head

Slowly sliding open

To the scent of oleander

The bad gushing out of you

Things in plain sight things hidden

It doesn't make any difference

If I could buffer my fall

Not with my body but my breath

Maybe stay awake for

The appearance of a small angel

Clear frozen beautiful

Like someone from Chicago

Living ocular proof

Of an immense force swooping

Swiftly downward to cool

The coils within coils

Having missed the free seminar

By several decades now

Even the namer of clouds is gone

So whatever I thought

Was tender or true

Left my face a network

Of hatchmarks from a mother

Lost in the exclusion zone

Father felled from the feet up

Son whose brown eyes

Are both sharper and softer

Than either of ours

An impossible child

No one could break or resist

Who has begun to beat his own

Diamondback path

To the edge of his fields

To the edge of his life

As the big clouds are rolling in

I try to herd the worst feelings

I ever felt the worst thoughts

The very worst under one

Warped sheet of metal

A nonbeliever dropped to

A pair of knobby knees

Every other thing reminds me

Of you even a tempera

By a seven-year-old

From Down Under titled

The Driver Sits in the Shade

But What About the Horse

It was something you might

Have said to a family waiting

For a taxi to the historic district

Or a gondola to take them

Off the mountain

Even a milk glass

Of field flowers sensed

You entering the room

Before you dropped me off

On a Lower East Side curb

With my rolling bags of grief

And pretty sheer brassieres

It's starting to seem as if everyone

Were already dead

And looking for my glasses

While Vic plunks out Buckets

Of Rain to a smoke-soaked

Roadhouse of rubes

My disappointment sits

Under the Tree of Disappointment

In a dirty skirt in a ruff

Of dirt the color of dirt

If a hand and it could be my hand

Moves over the bark it touches

Where an arrow passed through the trunk

The mind wills it into reverse

That the shaft of the arrow glide

Soundlessly backward

And the hand it could be your hand

Soothes the welt left by its entry

The air turns the blue of a seldom worn

Dress left in a closet by the woman

Who opened a notebook

To what must have been your hand

It looked like your striking

Script of course it was your hand

That wrote she doesn't get it

I was never there

Of my own volition

I would have never asked

The grass is strong unlike her

The water unperturbedly furled

The Ladder Tree leans toward me

And then swings out of reach

The ache that will last the rest

Of our lives stiffens into those words

The Tree of Knowledge

Tries to draw off the poison

Without destroying itself

Now who will make the record of us

Who will be the author

Of our blind and bilious hours

Of the silken ear of our years

Who will distinguish our dandruff

From the rest among the gusts of history

Who will turn our maudlin concerns

Into moments of incandescence

Who remember when I was a dirty blond

That hung like a mare's mane

A blond with an even dirtier mouth

And a pent-up anatomy

Your shoe trailing on the ground

Moving gracefully round me

Trying to stir up the hardpan

So thirsty and hot

Who fill us with the tingle

Of animation and of wonder

Who be there glistening

With sweat and forgiveness

Once the stall has been mucked

And re-mucked

The Tree That Owns Itself appears

Sickly but still blossoms

In Vic's hometown along with

The eight feet of earth round it

Which is not enough

Sedated to hopefully endure

The dozers and cranes

When the word turbine wanes

I can hear a bee entering a quince

A shoot of bamboo piercing

The skin of the earth

A black ant climbing a stem

The sound of raw umber

Distinct from burnt

The sound of still water

The sound of a towel

Drifting to the ground

The sound of you rubbing

Oil on someone else's limbs

It is so patently stupid to stick

By a one-stoplight-town dream

To love and be loved to the end

Without ruth or recrimination

Como una estúpida pelicula

We saw at an outdoor theater

In Guerrero standing up

From previews to credits

In a warm downpour

Then I see the quivery

Shadow of my stricken self

Left on a traffic island

At the noisiest intersection

In Buenos Aires

Drowning in the decibels

I don't want you to count

The conks on my trunk

Under the Tree of Conjugal Love

How this feels to be diminished

By one the one mistaken

For the one who would usher

Us away from the Tree

Of Failure and Shame

Beyond the Tree of Deceit

Unfulfillment and Illusion

Into the limbic woods

Of subtle adults-only stuff

Long-playing side-lit up-flickering

Beyond the Tree of Childish Wishes

Past the Tree of Ten Thousand Mistakes

I'm sure there is a word

In English there is always a word

What is that low-flying short-winged bird

Your mother would know

Even if she can't call up its name

They fly alone notwithstanding

They are abundant

But they fly only the breadth of a field

Traveling silently

It is early yet you said I'm going back to my study

A hand reaching toward your half-turned head

Pale sun filtering through the cloud floor

Passing over a tangle of tensions and angularities

A silver band suddenly visible in the grass

The perennials by the shed identifying

Themselves by vibration alone

The light discolored as candelabrum

From a preceding life your Junoesque

Hand turning the handle to a door carved

From a Tree of Tomorrows

Don't shut it I said We lack for nothing

Indissolubly connected

Across the lines of our lives

The once the now the then and again

C.D. Wright grew up in Arkansas and lives in Rhode Island and California. She is the author of over a dozen collections of poetry and prose and is a recipient of numerous awards, including a MacArthur Fellowship, the National Book Critics Circle Award, the Griffin International Prize, and the Lenore Marshall Poetry Prize. Her previous book is *The Poet, the Lion, Talking Pictures, El Farolito, a Wedding in St. Roch, the Big Box Store, the Warp in the Mirror, Spring, Midnights, Fire & All*. C.D. Wright unexpectedly passed away in her sleep on January 12, 2016.

With: After Thoughts

Nearly twenty years ago, I received a manuscript from C.D. Wright for the first time. We worked on nine books together, including this one and another that is forthcoming. Editing her was not a job, but rather an enduring conversation about the possibilities of poetry. It sustained me. Nonetheless, I could on occasion slip into a more reductive publisher's way of thinking, such as when I'd asked what we should call some of her recent works, which moved between poetry and prose, lyricism and reportage. "Prosimetric," she said and went on to school me in a long tradition of such writing, where poetry erupts out of the prose that surrounds it. Another time, as we were working on this book, *ShallCross*, she seemed to express concern—as any writer might—about whether anyone would read her, whether anyone would care. And her uncertainty came *not*, I believe, from vanity or ego or even resignation. She seemed instead to be thinking aloud, wondering how to make a place in the world for her type of writing and thinking. I assured her she didn't need to worry.

"Can you put words to an inchoate desire." That interrogative statement—one of a long list—appears toward the end of the last book that C.D. Wright lived to see published, *The Poet, the Lion, Talking Pictures, El Farolito, a Wedding in St. Roch, the Big Box Store, the Warp in the Mirror, Spring, Midnights, Fire & All*. The line is from "Questionnaire in January," a series of questions posed as affirmations. While no replies to the question-statements are given, it's evident that poetry is her resounding answer. "If I could buffer my fall / Not with my body but my breath / Maybe stay awake for / The appearance of a small angel."

Poetry was equally a verb to C.D.—and the absence of that question mark can be seen as an assertion that words *can* attach to such desire, that poetry *can* form and encourage, embody and identify desire. The answer to the implied question exists in the act of poetry itself. She *poems*. "It's a poem if I say it is."

Or, from an earlier book: "I poetry. I write it, study it, read it, edit it, teach it…" Her declaration was an act of resistance to assimilation. Poetry was her indictment of racism and ignorance, her celebration of the erotic, her way to impeach prosaic thinking and being. C.D. had formidable verbal energy, such pulsing genius, and so much desire upon which to latch her words: the desire to explore, to make a world of words, to hold herself and others accountable to being our best; the desire to do things right and challenge those who do not. She attached words to desire with an undeniable integrity, yet alongside her fierce convictions she wielded great humor.

I wish you hadn't
you down this
rabbit hole bec. I've
jumped down it too

At the time of Carolyn's death, we were finishing production on this book. As the editorial and design staff at Copper Canyon Press could tell you, she was exacting and determined in her choices, but those choices didn't feel forced or labored, were always brought forth in a spirit of collaboration.

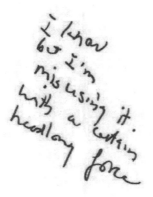

And this is the person I want to tell you about. From the moment when I first read that manuscript for *Deepstep Come Shining*, I entered into the privilege of being not only her editor but also her friend. I never saw her back down from her convictions, and I repeatedly witnessed her generosity. Her copyedited pages and proofs are full of her oftentimes hilarious notes; she would dance with all of us in the margins as we made her books: acknowledging a copyeditor's brilliance, self-deprecatingly scolding herself for verbal tics, gently disagreeing with me about titles, calling forth the sources behind her decisions, or simply asserting her particular voice and the provenance of that voice which brought her (and all of us who read her) here. To look back now at the notes she'd written in the margins of this and her other books, to witness the careful consideration and intention that went into every line, every word, every caesura, is to reinforce a voice that is already deeply situated in my ear. I was incredibly privileged to hear her, to read her, to learn from her. As a critic wrote: "Wright belongs to a school of exactly one."

After this death that was not supposed to happen, the outpouring of love for and respect of her has been profound. The shock of her passing and the grief so many of her readers feel is but testament to how deeply and thoroughly she influenced our lives. The depth of loss is testament to how much she was loved, as well as an indication of how much she valued others. She celebrated otherness. She was one with others. If I were limited to only one word to describe her, it would be the same word that ends this book's dedication to her husband and centers the title of her previous book of poems: *with*. Be with.

We're all there in her poems: strangers and friends, other poets and artists, the loving and the threatening, the famous and the unknown, the sacred and profane, the mother, the father, the son, the husband. She quotes an ever-expanding *us*. As I look at the proofs, with her scrawled notes, I'm brought back to that voice of hers, and thereby to the voices of all those whom she willed into her poems, her being. "Poetry's twin desiderata: to speak once and for all, to forever hold its peace. Like the old man said, 'Do I contradict myself? Very well then I contradict myself.'" Like the old man, Carolyn Wright contains multitudes. I read concern and anxiety and sadness and fear and anger in the poems of *ShallCross*. I also read love for a son and a husband, for friends and influences, love for words and their rhythms; and I in turn fall in love once again with a voice in love with the world and similarly loved by her readers. We become one with others through her singular voice:

Don't shut it I said We lack for nothing

Indissolubly connected

Across the lines of our lives

The once the now the then and again

thanks
for this

MICHAEL WIEGERS
EDITOR IN CHIEF
COPPER CANYON PRESS
FEBRUARY 2016

Poetry is vital to language and living. Since 1972, Copper Canyon Press has published extraordinary poetry from around the world to engage the imaginations and intellects of readers, writers, booksellers, librarians, teachers, students, and donors.

WE ARE GRATEFUL FOR THE MAJOR SUPPORT PROVIDED BY:

THE PAUL G. ALLEN
FAMILY FOUNDATION

Anonymous

Donna and Matt Bellew

John Branch

Diana Broze

Janet and Les Cox

Beroz Ferrell & The Point, LLC

Mimi Gardner Gates

Alan Gartenhaus and Rhoady Lee

Linda Gerrard and Walter Parsons

Gull Industries, Inc.
on behalf of William and Ruth True

Mark Hamilton and Suzie Rapp

Carolyn and Robert Hedin

Steven Myron Holl

Lakeside Industries, Inc.
on behalf of Jeanne Marie Lee

TO LEARN MORE ABOUT UNDERWRITING
COPPER CANYON PRESS TITLES,
PLEASE CALL 360-385-4925 EXT. 103

WE ARE GRATEFUL FOR THE MAJOR SUPPORT PROVIDED BY:

Maureen Lee and Mark Busto

Brice Marden

Ellie Mathews and Carl Youngmann as The North Press

H. Stewart Parker

Penny and Jerry Peabody

John Phillips and Anne O'Donnell

Joseph C. Roberts

Cynthia Lovelace Sears and Frank Buxton

The Seattle Foundation

Kim and Jeff Seely

David and Catherine Eaton Skinner

Dan Waggoner

C.D. Wright and Forrest Gander

Charles and Barbara Wright

The dedicated interns and faithful volunteers of Copper Canyon Press

The Chinese character for poetry is made up of two parts:
"word" and "temple." It also serves as pressmark for
Copper Canyon Press.

The poems are set in Adobe Caslon.
Printed on archival-quality paper.
Book design and composition by Phil Kovacevich.